THE NAME SPEAKS

ANGELA BROUSSARD

THE NAME SPEAKS

Doors Gates & Thresholds Book 1

Angela Broussard

3Trees Publishing
Gulfport, MS

The Name Speaks

© Angela Broussard 2021

www.silvercornerstone.com

angela@silvercornerstone.com

3Trees Publishing

2223 Beach Dr #903

Gulfport, MS 39507

3treespublishing@gmail.com

ISBN: 9781737019008

ISBN: 9781737019015 [ebook]

Cover Design: Laura Rivera-Rexach contact@designsxlaura.com

Editor: Heidi Cook heidi@heidicookstudios.com

Transcription: Gail Bishop

All rights reserved. This book is protected by copyright laws of the United States of America. This book may not be copied or reprinted for commercial gain or profit. The use of short quotations permissible with attribution to the author. Permission for larger segments granted upon request from Angela Broussard.

The Holy Bible, Berean Study Bible, BSB Copyright ©2016, 2018 by Bible Hub Used by Permission. All Rights Reserved Worldwide.

Scripture quotations taken from the (NASB®) New American Standard Bible®, Copyright © 1995 by The Lockman Foundation. Used by permission. All rights reserved. www.lockman.org

Scripture quotations taken from the Amplified® Bible (AMP), Copyright © 2015 by The Lockman Foundation. Used by permission. www.lockman.org

Scripture taken from the New King James Version®. Copyright © 1982 by Thomas Nelson. Used by permission. All rights reserved.

Institute for Scripture Research (ISR) The Scriptures 1998©. Used with permission.

Scripture quotations are from The Holy Bible, English Standard Version® (ESV®), copyright © 2001 by Crossway, a publishing ministry of Good News Publishers. Used by permission. All rights reserved.

CONTENTS

Acknowledgments	vii
Honor	1
Introduction	3
1. The Name	5
2. The Name and The Covenant	17
3. Whose Name is it Anyway?	25
4. An Uncanny Resemblance	31
5. A Name In Distress	35
6. Repairing The Breach	41
7. The Sound Redeemed	49
Glossary	53
Notes	55
About the Author	57
Doors Gates & Thresholds Series	59
The Destiny Series	61
Wells of SouthGate	63
3Trees Publishing	65
Kingdom Leadership Institute Gulf Coast	67
Designs by Laura	69

ACKNOWLEDGMENTS

From the earliest memory, numerous friends, acquaintances, and students have placed a demand upon me to put my words in print. The request that I write books detailing my adventures, and the plethora of teachings I've prepared over the years, has stirred me much. Desire to execute the task has been present, stemming from the depths of my relationship with Father God. I've maintained a belief that writing was part of my call and purpose for the cause of His Kingdom. Yet the attainment eluded me, save in blog form, a few local papers, and co-authored in-house publication of Bible Studies, until I met Rebecca Bennett. Serving the King and His Kingdom alongside Rebecca, and supporting her as she produced her own written work, provided a visible, tangible example of the task executed. I celebrated her accomplishment and became intimately acquainted with her process. *I witnessed someone finish a printed work.* This model demonstrated for me the path to take, revealing that I, too, could mature the daunting task. This is but one arena in which I am deeply grateful for her leadership and friendship. (A book needs writing of our adventures!) To the apostolic team of Crispin and Rebecca Bennett, I give honor. The region has been awaiting your arrival. Thank you for answering the call.

As powerful as Rebecca's example stands, I likewise acknowledge two influence of foundational import:

First, my mother. The student will encounter many paternal excerpts as examples in this series, therefore it is fitting to acknowledge the maternal lineage impact upon me.

Valeria Patricia, who sojourned a name mystery of her own, laid the bedrock of reading into the core of my being. Without this stable underlayment, I would not have been prepared for the arrival of a promised Bible from my Uncle Mickey in grade school. Of all the strengths my mother wove into my character, the gift of reading stands head and shoulders above the others. In terms of an inheritance, generations beyond us are postured in a state of betterment. Thank you, Mom, for investing in me, to invest in the future generations. I love you.

My English teacher, Ms. Luella Sedivy. Ms. Sedivy made a demand upon novice skills. She set about honing those skills into a purposed capacity to communicate orally, through the limbic system, and via the written word. Without question, Ms. Sedivy propelled me forward into a wordsmith position. To this day, I hear her correcting my sentence structure, or requiring clarity on a linguistic string. I am but one of numerous she touched in this way. At the time of this publication, Luella has transitioned to her reward before Father God. No doubt she has entered an awareness of the breadth of impact she has had for the Kingdom of God, tucked inside a high school classroom, situated in a little Nebraska panhandle town.

To speak of Ms. Sedivy, I must likewise acknowledge my beloved friend and distant cousin Brenda Terrell. Sharing a surname in our generations, it is now no surprise to me that the Terrell family provided a spiritual backdrop to my upbringing. Intertwined with our multiple adventures that included horses, toboggans, swing sets and three-wheelers, Brenda and I would forge hypothetical names for the future bevy of children we dreamed of having one day. That playful practice remained with me, serving as a formative structural component in my makeup. Names hold great import to Father God, and to me. I vividly recall the moment when Brenda accurately spoke to my teaching capacity. Her words were Father's purpose and destiny, breathing life into my heart. Thank you, Brenda.

Giving thanks to Anne Hamilton belongs here as honor. A broad statement of her meritorious impact can be found in the introduction to this series.

My husband has supported my spiritual pursuits minus complaint from the outset of our relationship. Gil, you've been the Steady to my Adventurous ways, and I am grateful. Your example of excellence and integrity has stood the test of time in our marriage, and I am the one refined by it. I needed this, not aware of it beforehand.

My children, Bethany, Tiffany, Aubrey, Israel and Keller, whom I purposefully, prayerfully, and calculatedly named: this work is the culmination of why your names were of great importance to me, back when what I perceived about naming and name covenant was small and indistinct. Your purpose and destiny is, most assuredly, hidden within the treasure of your names, and Father intends that you fulfill it, for the advancement of His Kingdom on the earth. As inheritors joined by generations, steward it with me? We are set for the work of the Kingdom and its King. I love you.

Dad, far from overlooked, you are the reason behind my pursuit. The broken places meant something incredibly valuable was stolen. The unresolved issue was not you; you were experiencing the symptoms of the unresolved issue. I found it!! It's fixed!! My love for you is unwavering. I accept you fully for who you are, and celebrate your life. The Repairer of the Breach had need of you. Valeria Annette and I are grateful.

To my editorial team I extend a deep gratitude. As structural framework to the process, you've been scaffolding of the highest caliber. My honor of our friendship has and will continue to be spoken of in tender celebration. Here, for all the world to see, I regard your professional capacity as excellent and integritous. May expansion be upon you. Thank you, Heidi Cook, Laura Rivera Rexach, and Gail Bishop.

HONOR

An old adage states "when the student is ready, the teacher appears." My discovery of Anne Hamilton's work might have been a fluke, had I not been specifically, determinedly, seeking answers to questions about my heritage. An uncanny longing to discover how a natural inheritance fit in the spiritual joint-heir position with Christ urged me forward. I held quest to trace out how the two components were to be expressed through my generational line, the history of which I knew little at that time.

Anne's work challenged me in Biblical study as no recent product had. Her merge of mathematical brilliance partnered with a Hebraic writing technique drew me as a moth to a flame. I experienced infuriating emotion at her writings' coy manner—deftly presenting cognitive content, simply to whisk it away, like a veritable hide-and-seek game.

The result? Fashioned after a Berean, I followed endnotes and links from beginning to end as she provided them. Not satisfied, I sought out the mouth of two or three witnesses to establish her words.

Rest assured, each component fleshed out as accurate. Anne moved to a trusted position, freeing me to work out the concepts for my personal journey, and in the course of employing the conclusions when necessary in ministry endeavors. The result? Deep breakthrough, major overturn, and marked freedom in each case applied.

. . .

The series you are about to enter is indebted to her untold years of legwork and hours of time spent on manuscripts fit for reading consumption. In no manner will this writing attain to the resplendent methods she employed to produce her life's work.

My expression will bridge the seasoned Bible student to her work, and provide a layer upon layer design of concept that marries effortlessly with the leadership training program, Kingdom Leadership Institute Gulf Coast, set into motion by Rebecca D. Bennett's Destiny Series. The training was birthed from the architectual design of the blueprints carried out by Wells of SouthGate, which the Bennett's founded. Further, it lays foundational groundwork for the maturing member of a local Ekklesia to be able to readily operate in Kingdom culture attributes.

<u>Name Covenant, Invitation to Friendship</u> and <u>God's Poetry, The Identity & Destiny Encoded In Your Name</u> by Anne Hamilton is recommended reading alongside this book to maximize your training.

Engage the entire series, implementing the strategies contained herein and prepare to enter your life's work as a Kingdom citizen.

INTRODUCTION

It is said that life is a journey, and we are pilgrims on it. Discovering your strengths, weaknesses and opponents on the journey exposes the reality of the spiritual realm ~ and just how fortified it is. Each book of Doors, Gates, and Thresholds will equip you to navigate successfully the unseen structural components of both the Kingdom of God and the kingdom of darkness, leading you to victory upon victory. The Kingdom of God awaits your choice and adjustment. Book One introduces the Master Poet, and His creation: you.

From this vantage, you will engage in the formation of your identity within the larger context of the Kingdom. As a Kingdom citizen, it is vital that you understand your role in service to the King. As Kingdom culture is introduced, you will have opportunity to walk through choice points (doors) and enforce the rule of the King (gates) at each progressive stage of your development (thresholds).

This series partners with instruction of the same series name for Kingdom Leadership Institute Gulf Coast. Whether in print or partnered with a live or recorded class, we will discuss your position of authority as a Christ One in terms of walking as He walked. May you produce maturity in His likeness–thirty, sixty, and yes, even one hundred-fold.

1
THE NAME

All scripture is given by inspiration of God, and is profitable for doctrine, for reproof, for correction, for instruction in righteousness

— 1 Timothy 3:16 BSB

Nestled deep in the linguistic heart of the Hebraic culture, scribes and scholars have studied the ancient Hebrew scriptures, seeking to know and understand the wellspring of wisdom that pours forth. This endeavor of discovery has journeyed many into a multi-layered learning experience, giving great credence to the Truth found in Hebrews 4:12.

The word of God is quick, and powerful, and sharper than any two-edged sword, piercing even to the dividing asunder of soul and spirit, and of the joints and marrow, and is a discerner of the thoughts and intents of the heart.

— Hebrews 4:12 KJV

The process of learning for any student will contain a series of steps or introductions to a concept or idea. Encountering a concept or idea merely one time rarely produces the full understanding or nuance of the matter. Thus, Hebrew scholars utilize a method of interpretation that allows for depth to be plumbed, wisdom to be obtained, and understanding to be mined. This method is called by an acronym: **PaRDeS**.

The western world uses the word *exegesis*, defined as, "the critical explanation or interpretation of a religious text,"[1] to refer to the study of the Bible. *Exegesis* stems from the Greek word meaning "to lead out," and by using it within our western mindset, a student considers historical background, cultural import, and complete manuscript context in order to arrive at a conclusion, or series of conclusions about the subject matter.

Our western model of thinking honors Greek philosophy with the carefully crafted and sterilized treatment of information. The western model allows the student to order concepts and ideas, folder them away, and retrieve the collection in their thoughts at a moment's notice. This approach is not wrong, per se. The quick treatment merely lacks the benefit of wonderment that lingering over the words of the Creator inspires. In contrast, the Hebraic form of *exegesis* honors the ancient texts by allowing reverence to lead and produces awareness that the words being handled are those of the Creator Himself.

As a word, PaRDeS has the meaning, "that of a garden, or orchard." The honor of interpretation lends itself to the garden origin, where the Creator shared intimate relationship with His creation. Leaning into Genesis, mental imagery easily makes room for conversation between the Creator and Adam. Their relationship was deepened by the social intercourse of ideas and the discovery of new concepts as they shared intimately. By observing, we can see it was in the garden that nuances were experienced. It was in the orchard that mature fruit developed from the deep. As the evening and the morning would boundary each day, the experiential knowledge of creation would widen and expand. The Creator's **sound** reverberated across the thread of all living. His **sound** would walk and engage, and He was known.

 ...they heard the voice of the Lord God walking in the garden in the cool of the day...

— Genesis 3:8 KJV

PaRDeS

For everything that was written in the past was written for our instruction, so that through endurance and the encouragement of the Scriptures we might have hope.

— ROMANS 15:4 BSB

How does Hebrew exegesis develop the depth of layers in learning? The four prongs of interpretation are found in the acronym:

1. **Pashat** = **plain**: the obvious and surface meaning.
2. **Remez** = **hint**: the deeper meaning, just beyond the literal.
3. **Derash** = **inquiry**: the comparative, sifted meaning.
4. **Sod** = **secret**: the meaning given through inspiration or revelation.

With each interpretive layer, deeper understanding develops. The **PaRDeS** method is similar to caramelizing an onion, in which flavors deepen with heat and over time, taking on a richness that adds to the final dish. This style of illumination brings the student to the harmonious living status of the Word, reflecting from itself complexities in simplicity, often hiding valuable gems in plain sight, not noticed upon first glance.

Peshat

The *peshat* layer is an anchor to Biblical interpretation. Prepared for a general audience, this level is typically readily accessible to any reader and produces an understanding of the literal observation, and the textual context, at face value. This plain representation answers the question,

> "What do we have to do?"

It can reflect either a figurative, symbolic or allegorical explanation as the keystone of Scripture. To discard the *peshat* of any passage is to lose its accurate and objective meaning.

Remez

The *remez* layer will hint at a significance beyond the literal expression, similar to an allusion. This can be symbolic, allegorical, or philosophical. Often the *remez* speaks of the content occurring before it. When the text has a repeated theme a short while after the original statement, this indicates a deeper meaning is present. *Remez* answers the question,

> "What is the reason or intent behind peshat?"

Remez is the content with which nobles, scribes, lawyers and judges interact. Psalms, prophecies, and Jesus' parables are examples of Scriptural text that can extend beyond the basic meaning it implies.

Derash

Derash means "to inquire of the Lord." This is a proper time to discover principles to apply to life. To *derash* is the responsibility of kings to uncover. When comparing two passages, one can sift a meaning of great value, like finding a kernel of wheat, after having threshed away the chaff.

> "How do we go about establishing the Kingdom of God?"

is the question this type of inquiry asks. Morals and 'rules to live by' are disclosed without denying the original meaning of the text.

Sod

The *sod*, or the secret meaning of a passage, will come forward through inspiration of the Holy Spirit or by revelation. This level retrieves mystery and honors the Words of the Creator as living and active. He brings forth new dimensions of understanding to those who engage His wisdom. The *sod* asks,

> "What Mystery of Christ is perceived here that drives what is happening?"

Discovery of meaning in this realm can occur individually, or corporately.

The secret things belong to the LORD our God, but the things revealed belong to us and to our children forever, so that we may follow all the words of this law.

— Deuteronomy 29:29 BSB

The Hebraic exegesis is suggested in four places in Biblical text, between the Old and New Covenant writings.

Whom would He teach knowledge? And whom would He make to understand the message? Those weaned from milk, those taken from the breasts! For it is: command upon command, command upon command, line upon line, line upon line, here a little, there a little.

— Isaiah 28:9-10 TS2009

But now, brothers, if I come to you speaking with tongues, what shall I profit you unless I speak to you, either by revelation, or by knowledge, or by prophesying, or by teaching?

— 1 Corinthians 14:6 BSB

...in order that He might give you, according to the riches of His esteem by power, to be strengthened in the inner man, through His Spirit, that the Messiah might dwell in your hearts through belief – having become rooted and grounded in love, in order that you might be strengthened to firmly grasp, with all the set-apart ones, what is the width and length and depth and height ...

— Ephesians 3:16-19 ISR

The Garden

The acronym, **PaRDeS,** as a word, is etymologically related to the English word paradise. Presented as *"garden"* in Song of Songs 4:13, the word is reflected as '*park*' in Ecclesiastes 2:5 and Nehemiah 2:8. As walking in a manicured and kept garden can be a visual and sensory delight, so also the Word of God offers a disciple as much desired–or as little desired- to satisfy an inner longing to know Creator intimately. As we journey through the series of Doors, Gates, and Thresholds, may you recognize the value in turning aside, lingering, and considering multiple facets of subject matter, in order to engage spiritual maturity. Like a veritable garden, we will plumb the depths, and journey into discoveries we may not have been prepared to find.

The Name

What's in a name? How do names impact our relationships with one another? Do names have any inherit power within themselves? Why was naming one of the first jobs Creator gave to His creation?

All of these questions, and more, have been asked through the ages as a matter of mere curiosity and as an intense search for deeper meaning. Language has served as the highest component of creation made in the image of Creator. As a sophisticated capacity endowed upon humanity, man would utilize breath and sound to create, express thought, and place import on the process of giving name to something. As humanity was created in His likeness, it stands to reason that communication would be foremost on His list of relational attributes to initiate.

Elemental Sound

Sound waves are the integral building blocks of all creation. Creator would speak, and things would *be*. Every species of mammal, reptile, or bird is equipped with the capacity to emit sound as a means to speak. Yet, of all His creation, one species has the essential assignment and prominent job of *naming*. The first Adam did so in a calculated joint venture with Creator.

This Creator-God was desirous of knowing and being known from the origin, the crowning days of creation's birth. He did not identify Himself directly by name to Adam, though they shared in a partnership of responsibility. Instead, He took a Presence-position, as Elohim, showing off His handiwork to Adam, inviting Adam to give identifiers to bird and beast.

And out of the ground the Lord God formed every beast of the field, and every fowl of the air; and brought them unto Adam to see what he would call them: and whatsoever Adam called every living creature, that was the name thereof.

— Genesis 2:19 NKJV

Deep, intimate knowledge of Creator was held in that paradise garden. It is after witnessing male and female expelled, that the Genesis student becomes aware of the naming process within the human species: *Adam, Eve, Cain, Able, Seth*...and so forth.

The task of naming turned from identifying creatures to identifying humanity. Naming, then, draws us into the story line and gives substance to character and behavior. Naming etches individuals on the heart and causes a relatable connection to form between two or more people.

It is here, within the sea of humanity, whether broken, flailing, failing, or succeeding, that Creator inserts Himself into the narrative, by name.

The Poet

Discovering the Creator who made the heavens and the earth in Genesis 2:4 opens a remarkable principle of sound that will follow us throughout this series. The written Hebrew language contains consonants and no vowels. Therefore, words can cross pollinate with meaning or connection. Many lexicons ignore exact-same Hebrew spellings because as they are spoken, a differentiation is made with vowels. In so doing, lexicons tell us Hebrew words have nothing to do with one another. However, as the Creator reveals Himself as a poet, we discover poetry makes connections through rhymes, puns and wordplay. Creator loves wordplay.

We are His workmanship, created in Christ Jesus unto good works which God has before ordained that we should walk in them.

— Ephesians 2:10 NASB

The Greek word for "workmanship," *poiçma*, means "to produce as in a creative expression,"[2] and by extension: poetry.

We are His poetic expression in the earth.

He Wants to be Known

Our Creator-God has a personal, proper name. It is a name set apart, different from all of the other names for God in the Bible. Many monikers, such as El, Elohim, and Baal share derivatives of sound and speech among false deities of ancient culture in some form. However, this personal name of God is not revealed openly until we meet Him with Moses in Exodus 3:12-15. The name He gives Himself?

'Ehyeh 'asher 'ehyeh.

'Ehyeh is the first-person form of the Hebrew verb meaning "to be," but the term reduced the phrase of words to the name *'Ehyeh*, or *I AM*, in verse fourteen. *Yahweh* seems to be an ancient version of the third-person form of "to be." The third-person reference may have been most suitable for Israelites considering their God.

Some scholars interpret *Yahweh* as a causative form like "He Causes To Be," but *'ehyeh 'asher 'ehyeh* favors a meaning like "He Is." Another way to say it? God told Moses, "I AM WHO I AM." Moses was to tell Israel, "I AM has sent me to you." Thereupon, I AM was communicated as,

> "Yahweh, the God of your fathers, the God of Abraham, the God of Isaac, and the God of Jacob ... This is my name forever."
>
> — Exodus 3:15 BSB

According to Rabbinical teaching, this name, Yahweh, otherwise known as "The Name," was so revered that the Jews simply wrote the four Hebrew consonants YHWH. The "four-hyphen letter" word was referred to as the Tetragrammaton. The Name, Yud-Hey-Vav-Hey literally means *"The Eternal and Self Existent One."*

Creator gives no formal introduction of Himself in the ancient text until His encounter with Moses. His name is, nevertheless, embedded in the Genesis account, rendered as haShem. Whenever the rabbis came across this sacred name in the text, they substituted another word for haShem, Adonai. Today, translators often render this as "THE LORD," using all capitals. Who was this Elohim, then, who created the heavens and the earth?

Shem

HaShem, as previously stated, was written by translators as THE LORD. All capital letters were used to distinguish His Name as THE NAME, referenced by the Tetragrammaton (YWYH). By removing this translation effect, we see wordplay emerge as we look for language connection.

Let us use the source text of Genesis 2:4 and 2:7 places where the word, *shem,* in various forms, is on display. *Shem* means "a mark or memorial of individuality; by implication honor, authority, character." In short, *shem* means, "name."

> *These are the generations of the heavens and of the earth when they were created in the day that the <u>LORD God</u> made the earth and the <u>heavens</u> ...*
>
> — GENESIS 2:4 BSB

> *And the Lord God formed man out of the dust of the ground and breathed into his nostrils the <u>breath</u> of life ...*
>
> — GENESIS 2:7 BSB

Were we to insert the Hebrew words, the phrases would look like this. (Note shem and sham are only differentiated by a vowel.)

> *In the day that the **haShem** made the earth and the* ha**sham**ayim ... ha**Shem** ... breathed into his nostrils the na**sham**ah of life ...

Poetry is more important to Creator than etymology. He's a poet, a word weaver, a name smith.

The nashamah—the action of HaShem to form life with breath[3]—is written multiple places in the ancient text. Here are but a few:

> *When You hide Your face, they panic; when You take away their breath, they die and return to dust. When You send Your Spirit, they are created, and You renew the face of the earth.*
>
> — Psalm 104:30 BSB

> *The Spirit of God has made me, and the breath of the Almighty gives me life.*
>
> — Job 33:4 NASB

> *...as long as my breath is still within me and the breath of God remains in my nostrils, my lips will not speak wickedness, and my tongue will not utter deceit...*
>
> — Job 27:3 BSB

> *By the word of the LORD the heavens were made, and all the stars by the breath of His mouth.*
>
> — Psalm 33:6 BSB

However, take note: nashamah—breathing—isn't the only action occurring as creation is taking place. *HaShem creates souls **through sound via naming**.* Creator didn't merely speak *words* to create the universe, He spoke *names*.[4]

> *He tells the number of stars. He calls them all by their names.*
>
> — Psalm 147:4 NKJV

Five Principles About Naming

Names are important. They cast a poetic vision for people and places. Sometimes, the root meaning of a name is significant, and sometimes it's about the wordplay. Names are as unique an identifier as a fingerprint from the Creator's perspective. Names call us forward into a future, depicting both call and destiny. Names attach us to both future and past, while serving as the border of our current experience.

Etymology is the study of the history or origin of words. These five principles will be used herein to search out the meanings and connections of names.

1. The etymological approach to the study of names can include root meanings and separate syllables.
2. Homological approaches attach similar sounds between structures or parts.
3. Anagrams, the rearrangement of letters, create new names.
4. Names by association can link one name to another.
5. An elision can be used to create new meaning when placed together, by the cutting or suppression of a vowel or syllable for the sake of meter.

As the PaRDeS method of exegesis will guide us through the series, so also will the naming principles above.[5] Set a focused intention to delve into the Word with a readiness to discover the impact of sound in fresh ways.

2

THE NAME AND THE COVENANT

The Merger

Ms. Luella Sedivy peered over the edge of her rimless spectacles and looked me straight in the eye.

"Do you know what your name means?"

Although I held a keen interest in names, I had to admit, I wasn't certain. I perceived I was about to find out.

"Messenger!" she retorted with a smile.

I turned my attention out the passenger window of the school van. Travelling across the Nebraska Sandhills into the Platte River Valley, we were on our way to the next speech and drama competition. The miles of open field and rolling plains made room for the thoughts that tumbled across the corners of my mind after the revelation.

An astute wordsmith, Luella commanded the English language with deft skill. Transferring her lauded capabilities to her high school students—who were less than enthusiastic about diagramming sentences—was her greatest gift.

Others in the van began to clamor.

"Do you know what my name means?" the jovial gaggle inquired, almost in unison.

Amid the noise, I reached up and touched the small cross pendant that sat upon a thin silver chain about my neck.

Miss Sedivy lowered her voice, so those in the back were less likely to hear.

"I've known your heart was tender toward the Lord for some time. That cross necklace said so."

In an instant, the two matters, my name and my faith, merged within my being. My heart yielded to the Spirit of God. The concept that my name meant "messenger" caused a light to flicker, like a pilot light inciting the flame on a gas burner. With little resistance, an awakening occurred.

Onoma

The element of sound is the origin point of the poetic, artistic expression of the Godhead. From the foundation of the world, the Creator breathed, releasing the sound of the name of every past, present, and future individual.

Names carry emotive content. They paint word pictures or bring forward a thought. Hearing the utterance of a name immediately causes one a mental image of the individual. A name includes one's rank, authority, excellence, or deeds. The Greek word for this phenomenon is *onoma*.

Onoma, pregnant with significance, is derived from a root word meaning, "to become acquainted with or to know."[1] To become acquainted with someone, or to know them, means that a deep understanding has occurred between two people. The very essence of another's personhood provides a backdrop for all interaction. The three components of onoma can be defined in this way: nature, character, and authority.

Nature

Rendered from its Latin root, *nature* means "born; produced."[2] Noah Webster, in 1828, defined *nature* as "the essential qualities or attributes of a thing." Those essential parts, or the 'essence' of a person are the observable and unobservable parts, including how a person interacts with others. Conveyed today as 'temperament,' we understand that essence describes what sort, or what particular, predisposition one owns.

Character

Character, then, draws from 'essence' and adds observable patterns. A *character* can be understood as "a mark, made by cutting or engraving, either by pen or stylus, on paper or other material."[3] Letters of an alphabet, numbers, and symbols are characters. Like those marks on a page, the character of a person is marked upon them through repeated testing and decision-making, which produces a reputation. By grouping a set of stable, distinctive, mental and moral qualities, one can identify the character of another.

Authority

Authority, that which is earned and not granted by birth, is the power derived from the influence of character and coincides with the rise of credibility, respectability, and dignity. These traits give the owner of earned authority the aptitude, or right, to act and give orders. When one exercises the power or command of their combined nature and character, their earned authority, or governing capacity is on display. With earned authority, self-governing capacity can be developed, a general can govern himself more than a sergeant. As one becomes apt at self-governing, the capacity to exert the influence of that authority over their realm of stewardship increases.[4] To walk in healthy authority, the nature and character of an individual must also be in health.

The Onoma of God's Name

They shall put My Name on the children of Israel, and I will bless them.

— NUMBERS 6:27 KJV

The fingerprint of God is upon every aspect of His creation via His Name. When *Ehyeh Asher Ehyeh*–the I AM–gave instruction to Moses, He made it clear that His Name was not simply going to convey who He was, but also who they were. In initiating the societal structure for a newly minted, out-of-bondage Israeli nation, I AM determined He would put His Name on them. They would literally carry His nature, character, and authority. **They would be like Him.**

> *In every place where I cause My Name to be recorded and remembered [through revelation of My divine nature] I will come to you and bless you.*
>
> — Exodus 20:24 AMP

I AM purposed to demonstrate Himself by means of a series of encounters, marked as a facet of His being, through the introduction of a new name for Himself at each juncture. How could He best express His likeness to another, without the benefit of intimate knowledge? The answer was found in onoma. **Names divulge the nature, the character, and the authority of the one who is known by them.**

The result of God's decision to be known by Egypt was that Moses advanced God's nature by His Name. Pharaoh encountered the I AM in an all-encompassing fashion. I AM put on display His complete authority over every false deity, the earth, and all created beings. Before every Egyptian, I AM showed an immense exhibition of power and might. Yet, when it came to His own, I AM instructed that a token of relationship be given: the mark of Covenant in the blood of the Passover Lamb on every door frame of each Hebrew family who desired to be delivered. Unlike the Egyptian, who lacked intimate friendship with I AM, the Hebrews received deliverance. They would be marked, and known, by His Name.

I AM set a precedent throughout the Old Testament of revealing Himself by employing various encounters. These encounters would show forth facets of His personhood by Name. As the young new nation tread through the wilderness, after being delivered from Egypt, the Godhead made Himself known by three specific name attributes:

1. **Jehovah Jireh:** the place of the Lord's provision
2. **Jehovah Nissi:** the Lord our banner
3. **Jehovah Rapha:** the Lord our Healer

Covenant Creator

I AM is the Source and Originator of both names and covenant. Adam, made in God's image, was given the honor of naming, just like God. Naming involved becoming acquainted with attributes and qualities; determining temperaments and behaviors. As a parent might thoughtfully consider on the name of a new child, so also Adam lingered over naming creation. This intimate knowledge surely gave way to grief when bloodshed was required, forming a covenant. After all, "if you name it, you become attached to it."[5] The animal skins in the Garden of Eden initiated one of many covenants in Scripture.

The Hebrew word for covenant is *beryith*. This word describes "the act of cutting, or passing between pieces of flesh."[6] Three of the most graphic examples of blood covenants sanctioned by I AM in the ancient texts are of Abram's encounter with I AM as He passed between the divided pieces of animal offerings, the Passover Lamb, and the act of circumcision. The graphic imagery reveals that covenants are not lightly undertaken. Moreover, covenant is considered legal language.

Greater and more powerful than a contract, a covenant transcends time and space. It remains in effect until it is fulfilled or overturned. Among Noah and Abraham, well known Covenant recipients, the cosmos, the earth, and the original garden also received pledges from the Most High.

Cutting Covenant

Why does God cut covenant? Cutting Covenant is a demonstration of the measure of His faithfulness. In the establishment of these covenants, He makes promises. I AM asserts to all humanity His desire to be in relationship with those fashioned in His image and likeness. Hebrews 6:13-20 expresses this intention.

> *God made a promise to Abraham because he could swear by no greater, he swore by himself. And he said, Surely in blessing, I will bless you, and in multiplying I will multiply you. And so after Jesus had patiently endured, he obtained the promise. For indeed men swear by the greater, covenant is always cut the greater to the lesser, and is an oath for confirmation to the end of all disputes. God determines to show more abundantly to the*

> *heirs of promise the immutability of His counsel. He confirmed it by an oath.*
>
> — Hebrews 6:13-20 KJV

In other words, He cannot lie. His guarantee stands. The Psalmist said it well.

> *My covenant will I not break, nor alter the thing that is gone out of my lips.*
>
> — Psalm 89:3 KJV

Father is inherently faithful.

> *Know therefore, that the Lord your God, he God, He is the faithful God, and He keeps covenant and mercy with those who love Him. He keeps his commandment even unto a thousand generations.*
>
> — Deuteronomy 7:9 NKJV

Before the foundation of the world, in the Artist's studio, Covenant and your name met upon the Table of Destiny. The *onoma* of God gave promise that His faithfulness would transcend generations, showing a glimpse of the importance of covenant. Whether you are aware or not, covenants under gird life. The grand question is: are you in the Covenant that fortifies blessing and supports your existence?

Everything rises and falls on Covenant.

Lives, governments, nations, relationships ... all things rise and fall upon covenant. In the western world, covenant is not widely utilized or discussed, but it exists in the fabric of culture. The closest example covenant in our society would be the marriage ceremony. The oft quoted passage of Scripture "the two shall become one"[7] denotes the very purpose of covenant: oneness. Typically, the bride will exchange her name for that of her groom. A civil record is created, making the legality of the spiritual or religious act known among friends, family, and governmental institutions. To dissolve a marriage, it is not enough to simply leave the relationship, as the defining parameters are still in place. A legal route must be applied.

The ancient eastern world engaged in the same legal proceedings; however, the process didn't necessarily take place at a courthouse. Transactions of covenant were conducted at the city gates, the door of a home or tent, the sharing of a meal or transfer of a commodity such as salt. Covenant transactions also included the exchange of names.

In Scripture, name covenants abound. Some are obvious; others are hidden or tucked away among the folds of a storyline or an encounter. The exchange of names were marks of friendship, faithfulness, and oneness.

3

WHOSE NAME IS IT ANYWAY?

On that fateful trip to the speech and drama competition with Ms. Sedivy, my name merged with purpose and destiny and catapulted me forward into expressing the nature my name projected.

It is no different for you. Upon your name is embedded, and within your name is hidden, your call, your purpose, and your destiny within the kingdom of God. How are you designed to be impinging upon the kingdom of darkness? In what manner are you called to come before and answer unto the King of Kings and to receive from Him that which you are to be releasing in this realm?

Your Name

At the sound of your name, all creation hears and recognizes your identity. Within your identity is contained the projected path the Father of all creation purposed for you upon His Table of Destiny, where Covenant and Name met: your calling. With the blueprint of your Original Design intact, your identity, expressed through your spirit-man, directs you into the spiritual work of the Kingdom of God.

It is with this understanding that we present ourselves as instruments of righteousness to God.

Named by The Name

You were named by The Name, not simply the Tetragrammaton (YHWH), not simply Hashem, but: *'Ehyeh Asher 'Ehyeh* - I Am that I Am. I Will Be what I Will Be. Embedded in Genesis 1:1, Father God revealed His movement, revealing Himself: *'Ehyeh, Hashem, Yahweh.*

'Ehyeh said to the Levitical priesthood, *"you will put My Name upon the children of Israel and I will bless them."*[1] Both natural Israel and spiritual Israel, those grafted into the Vine as sons of God, were designated to carry His Name. His Name is upon us. It's unto His Name that we must give account. The Name depicts His nature, His character, and His authority. In giving His name, Father gave His Covenant. Because He is an eternal and faithful God, He brought about a covenant—the cutting that produced blood after Adam committed high treason. This first sacrificial act produced the clothing by which Adam and Eve would be covered. That covenant provision brought forward the covenant law down through the generations to the nation of Israel.

Covenants are eternal. They are powerful. A covenant remains in force until it is fulfilled. Covenants are greater than contracts and deeply involve relationships. Our covenant keeping God wants to get to know us. He introduces Himself through His Name. Drawing us, He leads us to the opportunity of a name covenant so that He can fulfill the call that He's embedded in the DNA that drives our life.

> *Before I formed you in the womb, I knew you; before you were born, I consecrated you. I have appointed you a prophet to the nations.*
>
> — Jeremiah 1:5 ESV

When Jeremiah came forth crying from the womb, embedded within him was the call of God inside his name. Jeremiah means: the Lord loosens and throws; elevated of the Lord, appointed.[2] From a very young age, the ministry of Jeremiah began. Moved by His relationship with God, his words made an impact upon nations. The Scriptures contain but a small sliver of understanding as to the depth of influence he had upon the nation of Israel and neighboring kingdoms. Jeremiah walked and moved in the fulfillment of his call as he stepped into nation after nation, releasing the word of the Lord through the Torah, the Covenant treatise of his day.

Eternal Covenants

Covenants that are cut in the kingdom of God transcend time and space. Father Himself will fulfill His portion of the agreement. Yet, there are covenants made in and with darkness that are equally spiritually eternal, made by a created being attempting to usurp the authority of Creator God.

The eternal nature of covenants predicates a reality: dark covenants may be hidden in ones' generational lineage. An unholy covenant, having been forged in a family via the actions of a member of a previous generation may utilize character weakness. This may show up as a proclivity toward besetting sins, in which the individual simply cannot gain mastery over - and, the use of the elemental sound of your family name. Isaiah discusses these unholy agreements:

> *Because you have said, 'We have made a covenant with death, and with Sheol we have made a pact. The overwhelming scourge will not reach us when it passes by, for we have made falsehood our refuge, and we have concealed ourselves with deception...'*
>
> — Isaiah 28:15 NASB

Since a covenant is forged between two parties, the Greater and the Lesser, a dark covenant fused with a counterfeit god produces a captivity in which one is helpless to dislodge the structure that the enemy has built into a life, and over a name. According to Irish history, this is called a *geas*.

Enter the wisdom of God: a plan to confound the kingdom of darkness, because an unholy covenant can only be undone by a greater, righteous covenant. Isaiah continues in verses 16-18:

> *Therefore thus says the Lord GOD, "Behold, I am laying in Zion a stone, a tested stone, a costly cornerstone for the foundation, firmly placed. He who believes in it will not be disturbed. I will make justice the measuring line and righteousness the level; then hail will sweep away the refuge of lies and the waters will overflow the secret place.*

Your covenant with death will be canceled, your pact with Sheol will not stand ..."

— Isaiah 28:16 NASB

This greater covenant was ratified in the person of Jesus Christ when He fulfilled the action as the Lamb of God slain from the foundation of the world. As His blood came upon the earth, it legally reversed the dark covenant that the first Adam had made in treason. The provision was made to overturn any and all unholy agreements from that point forward.

Covenants are expressed in different forms. Multiple types of covenant are discovered within Scripture. Of particular importance to humanity are those that govern our relationship with Father, and how we become partners in His Kingdom purposes. The Blood Covenant governs our spiritual life, and serves as an entry point in which we partake of the Spiritual Kingdom. The name covenant, threshold covenant, salt covenant, and the peace covenant all pertain to our progression in this Christ life - our purpose and destiny.

A name covenant is all about friendship. It's about faithfulness. It's about devotion.[3]

This begs the question:
Whose name is it, anyway?

Geas

This tidbit of Celtic history produces a concept pertinent to our conversation about the ownership of names. To hold one prisoner, based upon the failure to complete a vow or pledge, was called a *geas*. The spirits of darkness are empowered by a person not fulfilling an agreement, which results in captivity. The eternal nature of covenants and the creativity within elemental sound by Father merges upon humanity's action of naming and the spiritual captivity produced by a geas.

Ownership of names, while under God's creative unction, may have been hijacked by the unsuspecting action of an ancestor, without regard to the true spiritual nature of the pledge created in circumstances driven by superstition.

Held captive by the sound of your name?

Such a concept need not be considered out of the range of possibility. After all, iniquity and transgression impact the land, therefore it stands to reason that sound can be bent, or perverted by captivity. Further, given this awareness, it becomes easy to understand that the genus-loci, or spirit of a place[4], is directly impacted by the movement of people across geographical locations, through elemental sound. This impacts landmarks, cities, regions, and nations.

How can one ascertain if there is a geas attached to the elemental sound of a name? Are there any markers that clearly identify a captive place upon a person's life? How might such an imprisonment of sound be noticed? As Anne Hamilton states in her writing:

There is no name so negative it cannot be redeemed; no name so positive it cannot be corrupted; no name about which we can assume unadulterated holiness for ourselves or any member of our family; no name where we can sit back in relief and decide nothing needs to be done.[5]

She further iterates succinct geas markers, and presents them. The following list of characteristics, circumstances, or spoken words are likely not exhaustive, but certainly are a strong starting point of discovery:

- Self mutilation or cutting
- Birth via Cesarean section
- Stockholm Effect
- One feels like a hostage without supporting evidence
- Inability to use gifts or talents except in restricted ways
- Repeated identity theft
- Severely restricted movement
- No fear of death
- "I did it my way" or "I am my own man/woman"

These circumstances, particularly when more than one can be identified, may very well point to a *geas* having been placed upon the elemental sound of a name. Further, Anne's research identified the names with the variants below particularly susceptible to the potential of captivity, based on historical references within the Gaelic history:

- Gil - [Gilbert, Giles, Jill, Gillian]
- Kil - [Kyla, Kileigh, Killan, Kyle]
- Car - [Karen, Kara, Caroline]
- Cor– [Corey, Courtney, Corby]
- Val– [Valerie, Valda, Valentine,]
- etc...

Once again, we must ask the important question: in pursuing your purpose and destiny embedded within your name, *just whose name is it, anyway?*

4

AN UNCANNY RESEMBLANCE

Ms. Sedivy impinged spiritual import upon my existence the day she married my name with the God-call upon my life. Empowered by the strength of that revelation, I would walk many years fulfilling the premise of the Gospel, merging the wisdom of the Word with a natural propensity to influence others. My press sought to lead others toward developing a viable relationship with the Godhead, in order to become a productive member of the Kingdom of Righteousness.

It had never occurred to me that my name meant any more or less than "messenger," and certainly I attached the messenger moniker to faith in Christ. Yet, my life became cluttered with ups and downs, and a series of circumstances plagued my path. Therefore, when confronted with the possibility that my name had somehow been apprehended in history by the kingdom of darkness, I determined to investigate. Using the thought process I'd been introduced to by Anne, it took less than one minute for my jaw to drop from amazement at what my internet search revealed. Reading the first line of content from query number one, a series of flashbacks connected multiple historical events for me. The truth of Anne's words, that no name was free from the possibility of being hijacked, washed over me like a punch in the gut. I steadied myself, focusing on Father God. As quickly as the stunning blow had come, the Holy Spirit moved just as fast to remind me: Jesus had paid the price for this usurp of sound. My name—Father's name for me—could be offered back to Him for cleansing, and His ownership retrieval.

The interesting thing about linguistic origin, and the subsequent mythology of a region is that it can oft reveal the spiritual forces of darkness operating in and through a people group of the era. I offer my name as a resident example of how ideas and concepts are entrenched in names.

- **Angela**
- **Meaning:** Angel; Messenger, Bringer of Truth
- **Name origin:** Greek
- **Attached Mythology:** In Greek mythology, Angelos (Ancient Greek: Ἄγγελος) or Angelia (Ἀγγελία) was a daughter of Zeus and Hera who became known as a chthonic deity. Angelos was raised by nymphs to whose care her father had entrusted her. One day she stole her mother Hera's anointments and gave them away to Zeus' consort Europa. To escape Hera's wrath, she had to hide first in the house of a woman in labor, and next among people who were carrying a dead man. Hera eventually ceased from prosecuting her, and Zeus ordered the Cabeiroi to cleanse Angelos. They performed the purification rite in the waters of the Acherusia Lake in the Underworld. Consequently, she received the world of the dead as her realm of influence, and was assigned an epithet katachthonia ("she of the underworld").

As I read the storyline that was associated with this Greek goddess, a cold, clammy realization overtook me. While the myth seemed far removed from reality, I could quickly detail an uncanny resemblance to the storyline. Keynotes stood out to me: Theft, independence, infidelity, friendship with consorts, midwifery training, death, and the power of influence. I could confirm that similar scenarios had been my lot, albeit not in the form of myth. Surely these events could plague any individual, but with such precision? I furthered my search, using first and last name as well.

When I held this matter next to the list of ways in which a *geas* appeared to be in place upon the elemental sound of my name, I squared my shoulders. I now had evidence that my lengthy journey to step into my life's work had been surruptitiously plagued by the enemy. Like a computer operating system or program, running in the background of my life unawares, he was staking claim on my gifts, talents, and abilities. I wasn't sure how he had gained legal right just yet, but I had enough work to do at the moment.

Gathering all my notes, I stepped into the prayer closet, and purposed before Father that I wanted the ownership of my name to belong to Him alone. I set out to untangle the elemental sound of my name from the unholy covenants, myths, and pledges that had been assigned to the sound of it.

5

A NAME IN DISTRESS

If the foundations be destroyed, what can the righteous do?

— Psalm 11:3 KJV

For the Hebraic culture, naming is about conception: the origin of a matter; the onset of a journey. Thus, determining the identity of a babe brings honor to the value of life, as it sounds the call, the purpose; the destiny for that child.

Would we be astonished to discover that numerous times children are given a name based on unresolved issues in the family line? The pattern in Scripture peeks out at us in *remez* fashion. It's easy to see the deeper meaning, once pointed out. We begin our conversation in Genesis 41, looking closely at the name covenant created at the onset of Joseph's season of nationwide leadership in Egypt, immediately after he accurately interprets Pharaoh's dream.

Joseph Is Made a Ruler

Then Pharaoh said to his servants, "Can we find a man like this, in whom there is a divine spirit?" So Pharaoh said to

> Joseph, *"Since God has informed you of all this, there is no one as discerning and wise as you are. You shall be in charge of my house, and all my people shall be obedient to you; only regarding the throne will I be greater than you."* Pharaoh also said to Joseph, *"See, I have placed you over all the land of Egypt."* Then Pharaoh took off his signet ring from his hand and put it on Joseph's hand, and clothed him in garments of fine linen, and put the gold necklace around his neck. And he had him ride in his second chariot; and they proclaimed ahead of him, *"Bow the knee!"* And he placed him over all the land of Egypt. Moreover, Pharaoh said to Joseph, *"Though I am Pharaoh, yet without your permission no one shall raise his hand or foot in all the land of Egypt."* Then Pharaoh named Joseph Zaphenath-paneah; and he gave him Asenath, the daughter of Potiphera priest of On, to be his wife. And Joseph went out over the land of Egypt.
>
> — Genesis 41:38-45 NASB

Upon receipt of the accurate dream interpretation, the Egyptian ruler demonstrated his gratitude to Joseph. Speedily positioning the Hebrew as a valued advisor, Pharaoh's response produced three changes to the former prisoner's state of being: advancement, an honorary membership to the royal house, and a name covenant.

The three exchange points Joseph experienced correlate the three relational benefit markers of covenant: that of shared identity, resource, and enemy. The foe in this scenario is the famine. The symbols of identity and resource are: the signet ring, or sign of authority, placed upon Joseph's hand; the dignity of identity found in Pharaoh's mantle; and notably, the receipt of *a new name*.

This new name, as commonly interpreted means: "a revealer of secrets," or, "The man to whom secrets are revealed."[1] Yet a Hebraic transliteration of *Zapenath-Paneah* spectacularly unveils Joseph's calling, purpose, and destiny in definition as: "stored beautiful rest."[2]

Entrance into the royal household would not be conclusive without the political and religious alignment of marriage. The former Hebrew slave married the daughter of the high priest of the false deity On. Joseph's new wife, *Asenath*, named after the Egyptian goddess of wisdom, was, in all likelihood, dedicated at birth to the god her father served, as her name meant: "Who Belongs To Neir."[3]

Pharaoh employed word-play via *Zaphenath* and *Asenath* with the covenant act of marriage, in all probability to increase the wisdom in the lineage of those affiliated with On.

Joseph was now in every respect immersed in the culture of his captivity. We find no evidence in the ancient text that Joseph deviated from his practice of worship to the Most High God. The continued account suggests that Joseph was an influence on the culture, rather than absorbed by it. By creative license, it is easy to consider that Joseph, for all the joy of fulfilling his childhood dream, yet held heartache and a deep longing for the broken places of his history. *If the foundations be destroyed, what can the righteous do?*

Joseph, in all probability, prayed much and often. The breach created by his immature response to the dreams of his youth, and the resulting behavior of his brothers must've plagued his thoughts regularly. A curious discovery emerges as Joseph fathers a family of his own. The sibling related, unresolved familial issues he struggled with appeared in the choice of name for his firstborn. Yet, the greatest grief tucked deep within Joseph's heart was the loss of his mother.

The Sons of Joseph

> *Now before the year of famine came, two sons were born to Joseph, whom Asenath, the daughter of Potiphera, priest of On, bore to him. Joseph named the firstborn Manasseh; "For," he said, "God has made me forget all my trouble and all of my father's household." And he named the second Ephraim; "For," he said, "God has made me fruitful in the land of my affliction."*
>
> — Genesis 41:50-51 NASB

The text communicates the explanation behind the names of these boys, poignant as they are. Through elemental sound, we find the connection between *EPHRiam*, meaning *doubly fruitful*, and the geographic area of Benjamin's birth and Rachel's passing: *EPHRathah, to be fruitful, or to bear fruit.*[4]

Jabez

Joseph's history wasn't the only that showed up in family monikers. Other familial issues can be traced to the naming process of many.

Among them, Abraham and Issac produced Jacob in a plot of deceit to avoid death. Gideon produced Ambimelech after struggling with false humility and ego. David's history was dotted with numerous Jonathan's of varying character as a deafening reminder of broken covenant and relational breach among the tribes of Israel. Among these, and a plethora of others, however, a gem of a moment of name redemption glints and gleams from it's position in Scripture, and is worthy of our attention:

> *Jabez was more honorable than his brothers, and his mother named him Jabez, saying, "Because I bore him with pain." Now Jabez called on the God of Israel, saying, "Oh that Thou would bless me indeed, and enlarge my border, and that Thy hand migh be with me, and that Thou wouldst keep me from harm, that it may not pain me! And God granted him what he requested.*
>
> — 1 Chronicles 4:9-10 NRSV

Many are familiar with the prayer of Jabez, thanks to a popular Christian book written by Bruce Wilkinson. The author effectively takes a reader through the process of evaluating one's own *onoma*: nature, character, and authority. The encouraged result of considering Jabez' prayer is to pray similarly. Such a prayer can overturn any dark proclivity caused by broken or unholy covenant, and restore a believer to a path marked by God's covenant blessing.

Jabez stands as a definitive Scriptural example of seeking Father's ownership over a given name. The passage says it all: Jabez was named "pain child" literally, as the birthing process was so traumatic to his mother!

We are not given the name of Jabez' mother, although scholars do consider him of the lineage of Caleb, the son of Coz, or Kenaz.[5] His difficult birth is similar to the birth of Benjamin, the younger brother of Joseph, born to Rachel. The account of Benjamin's birth reveals that as Rachel departed, she named her son *Ben-oni,* that is: *son of my sorrow.* However, Jacob quickly restated the child's name *to son of my right hand.* The quick action of Jacob predates the Mosaic law concerning the vows of wives and daughters,[6] but discloses the cultural practice as having redeeming merit, so that untoward words spoken can be annulled. Like the geas of Celtic taboo might hold one captive, so also, for Jacob to allow a vow, or in this case, a name pronouncement of negative impact, by a woman in his household to stand would mean it must be honored. Thus, Jacob quickly moved to rename the child.

There is no evidence that Jabez' father did the same for him. Given the straightforward manner in which the Biblical text speaks of his birth, it is no small stretch to consider he was a breech-positioned baby, or that perhaps the mother labored many difficult days. While the Hebraic structure of the name Jabez does give rise to question the exact meaning,[7] there is likelihood that persecution was associated with the name. After all, if you spent your entire life being called "pain" wouldn't you desire to have a different greeting when you entered a social gathering? Jabez honorably approaches God, and effectively requests that his life be not as his birth, constricted, or constrained in any way.

Jewish scholars indicate that Jabez was an eminent doctor in the law, whose reputation drew many scribes around him. A learning center developed, a town called by his name:

The families of scribes who lived at Jabez were the Tirathites, the Shimeathites, and the Sucathites ... Those are the Kenites who came from Hammath, the father of the house of Rechab ...

— 1 Chronicles 2:55 KJV

Scholars note the development of his public service, talents, and distinguished worth in later life. This gives rise to the belief that God had indeed answered his prayer, just as it is recorded in Scripture. Similar to that of Jacob,[8] Joseph's father, Jabez demonstrated sincerity of faith in God to overturn the negatively spoken moniker into a name of blessing. In making a vow and in redeeming his name, his actions reflect those of Jacob upon Rachel's death.

The Psalmist David expressed a sentiment similar to that of Jabez. Psalm 139:5 states:

[You] are acquainted with all my ways. Even before there is a word on my tongue, Behold, Lord, You know it all. You have encircled me behind and in front, And placed Your hand upon me.

— Psalm 139:5 NASB

Yet the most beautiful render of the request of Jabez' heart, reflected in David's song is found in The Passion Translation of the Bible:

You are so intimately aware of me, Lord. You read my heart like an open book and you know all the words I'm about to speak before I even start a sentence! You know every step I will take before my journey even begins. <u>You've gone into my future to prepare the way, and in kindness you follow behind me to spare me from the harm of my past.</u> With your hand of love upon my life, you impart a blessing to me. This is just too wonderful, deep, and incomprehensible! Your understanding of me brings me wonder and strength.

— Psalm 139:5 TPT

6

REPAIRING THE BREACH

 And they that shall be of thee shall build the old waste places: thou shalt raise up the foundations of many generations; and thou shalt be called, The repairer of the breach, The restorer of paths to dwell in.

— Isaiah 58:12 KJV

Hope Arrives

Jesus stepped into a prestigious call when He became the Ultimate Repairer of the Breach. His primary function as Repairer of the Breach fixed the first Adam's violation of stewardship duty of the earth.

What does it mean to be a repairer of the breach? A *breach* is a broken place, like a wall once positioned as protection. Used as a legal term, breach is defined as: *The violation of a law; the violation or non-fulfillment of a contract; the non-performance of a moral duty; the non-performance of duty, being a breach of obligation, as well as a positive transgression or violation.*[1]

Covenant is a legal transaction, and breaking or violating covenant results in a breach.

When Jesus repaired the legal breach of the first Adam, He reestablished our relational connection to Father. This tremendous benefit wasn't a one time investment! The cleansing power of the Blood of the Lamb is accessible at any moment, through repentance, renunciation, and forgiveness.

> *If we confess our sins, he is faithful and just to forgive us our sins, and to cleanse us from all unrighteousness.*
>
> — 1 JOHN 1:9 KJV

As Repairer of the Breach, Jesus, The Word, re-established His authority and ownership of the sound of His Name, dethroning those who had usurped various titles. Deities and godlings in His era were effectively stripped of their squatter's rights. Mithra had illegally claimed the title of the goddess of light. Jesus took back the name as He unequivocally stated, "I AM the Light of the World."[2] His words were not spoken in the dark or in hidden places. They were openly conveyed as a demonstration of responsibility as the Bearer of The Name. Jesus became our example beyond Jabez into the New Covenant,[3] that the righteous meaning of our names must be redeemed or repaired.

Nonetheless, free will allows mankind to sin. Rebellion to God continues to this day. Individuals may purposefully forge a pledge or covenant with the kingdom of darkness. Others engage in entanglement with the unholy. Entering unholy covenants is an illegal act. Such behavior requires repentance as the condition to remove the legal holding point of the enemy.

Geas

Transgression, iniquity and sin fractures agreement with the Covenant Creator.[4] To participate in holy covenant with our Creator, only to turn and break the terms of that pledge, creates a legal breach, and provides a holding point for the enemy.

A solo item of transgression, repented of, does not necessarily a demonic stronghold make. Patterns of iniquitous behavior cause such a hiding place. In addition, the enemy will use trauma markers, or wounds, to attach spiritual forces of unholy intent in a person's life.

The satan is engrossed in undermining humanity, seeking to keep an individual from entering their full stature and position as a Kingdom citizen. He will apply great deception to hide his ambition, quietly ensnaring his victim, and retreating to a refuge of darkness. He operates his schemes of defilement from the safety of obscurity. He does not work alone, as a host of fallen spiritual creatures join him in his rebellion. Remember how the prophet stated it? The rebellious fallen beings declare, *"we have made falsehood our refuge, and we have concealed ourselves with deception ..."*[5]

Given that the enemy prefers to operate under the cloak of darkness, what evidence would reveal the existence of his strongholds?

One may experience a challenge with besetting sins or a pattern of inability to overcome untoward behavior. In addition, a thorough personal assessment of the following items, in any context, oft proceeds a discovery period, that may lead to the disclosure of a *geas*.

1. **Repression:** the sense that one's life is *restricted or limited by someone or something, either by force or by exercise of authority*
2. **Regression:** *a return to earlier stages of development*
3. **Suppression:** the experience of intentional *exclusion from consciousness of a thought or feeling.*
4. **Depression:** *a persistent feeling of sadness and loss of interest in life*
5. **Oppression:** the experience of *prolonged cruel or unjust treatment or control*
6. **Obsession:** *the state of being overly fascinated with someone or something.*

Whether vague or highly detailed, symptoms such as these point toward a plot of the satan. His greatest win would be full ownership of the created child, the person God formed to fulfill His purpose in the earth! When unrighteous patterns are present, the prince of the power of the air is to be suspect. Our actions break covenant and make us vulnerable by giving legal right to the powers of darkness.

The single remedy, the one we've previously discussed, is that of the blood-red ink of the Lamb of God, poured out from the cross, ratifying a new legal decree of freedom. The legal provision of the New Covenant was prepared for the breach-points. After removing the legal claim of the enemy through repentance and renunciation, it is necessary to apply the blood of Jesus to that broken place. This is the arrival of our Hope.

The Sound of History

Henry Harvey brushed his weathered hand across his heavy brow, lifting the edge of his hat slightly as he did so. Framed by sun-kissed, wrinkled, yet velveted leather-like skin, his dark eyes pierced the distance. As far as his eye could see, the Nebraska landscape presented promise. The soil spoke directly to his pioneering spirit, reverberating the echo of his pioneering forefathers.

The sound was irresistible. This caused him to consider the formidable task ahead. His heart was spry, but the years leaned heavy into his frame. In order to break up fallow ground, he'd need help.

The best course of action would be to open ground with his oldest son, Albert Austin. Albert was familiar with the labor required, and not soft, as his youngest brother, Sidney, twenty years his junior, seemed to be. The women would have their portion to contribute.

In a few years, Henry and Albert would bring the land to full productivity. It would be a wise investment, and allow Henry Harvey to leave a suitable inheritance to Albert.

"A good man leaveth an inheritance to his children's children..."[6] Henry Harvey muttered under his breath.

The Bible had become his constant companion. The faith of his fathers finally settled deep into his spirit after the loss of two of his children in infancy. Of the remaining sibling group, the girls outnumbered the boys, and the baby, Sidney was doted upon. Albert, however, knew his father's work ethic, and mirrored it. He would merely have to agree to relocate from Goshen County.

Henry Harvey reached again to the brim of his hat, and squared his jaw. Legacy was on the line. He would hesitate no longer. The invitation to Albert rose with purpose, and with a deep resonating sound, Henry offered his best to his offspring.

Rarely in today's modern society, do we experience family history handed down verbally. Stories, anecdotes, historical accounts and remembrances of honor are of a bygone era, replaced by technology and fast paced, independent living. As a result, the initiating issue of captivity in a family line may be hidden. This is no surprise! It is exactly how the powers of darkness intend for them to be.

Family anecdotes of generations past have the power to reveal clues. For instance, one may grow up hearing the "family story" about "Aunt Bonnie" and "Uncle Clyde" going on a crime spree marked by murder and theft. Their child, your cousin, struggles with kleptomania and harbors fantasy of taking the life of others. The connection in this hypothetical example is stark and palpable. It identifies a generational link of iniquity. The unholy kingdom would like to exploit the lack of repentance on holding points of iniquity in the previous generation, by continuing the activity in a new generation.

By identifying symptoms, a root cause may surface through process of elimination. The prayer closet is the place to begin discovery. Father God knows your ancestry. He is pointedly aware of who-did-what on your generational line, and is competent to bring such information forward. The Holy Spirit is a capable strategist, and can be trusted to instruct how to proceed, once a cause is determined.

In every generation, one arises with a call upon their life to repair the broken places. Each have opportunity to pass the test and overcome fault of the preceding generation. Diligent work in the prayer closet can steadily untangle each revealed point of captivity. Partnering with Father, new boundaries can frame a new place. A fresh foundation, established in righteousness, coupled with faithful commitment to covenant, can change the trajectory of a dynasty.

In my case, upon introduction to the folklore attached to my first name, the captivity point was on my paternal last name. What had given access to the enemy? A stolen inheritance.[7] A real life Esau and Jacob scenario set a dam at the annex of a tributary of familial blessing once flowing wide open.

Broken Promises, Stolen Inheritance

For many years, the arrangement ran perfectly. The plan to prepare an inheritance for his family, properly appointed to his oldest son hummed along without a hitch. Seasons of seedtime and harvest led to the establishment of the farm. Sowing and reaping continued unabated until the fateful day that Henry Harvey's wife passed away. It was a blow to the entire family, yet Henry Harvey found love again, in the arms of a woman named Belle.

Belle and her daughter Ida, opportunists, managed to weave their way into the hearts of the oldest and youngest, as Ida soon married the baby of the family, Sidney, shortly after Henry Harvey and Belle tied the knot.

Albert Austin watched from the shadows, concern mounting within, as he witnessed Belle's maneuvering ways. He never laid down his work ethic, and continued to labor, establishing and expanding the home place, purposed in his position as first-born inheritor. At the time of his father's passing, he would stand as patriarch of the family, and the responsibility of the betterment of all would rest squarely on his shoulders.

Yet, as Albert worked, he grew steadily uneasy, catching whispers on the wind, caught by the breeze, moving through the kitchen window in the cool of the morning, or close of the day. Belle and Ida held a secret; a conniving intention to usurp the wealth created by father and son, respected and regarded members of the small community. The hard earned inheritance was on the line, and Belle would be certain to position her darling daughter's future. Using Sidney as the pawn of her plan, Belle began intimating to Henry that Sidney was in better position to carry on the family legacy.

Day unto day, night unto night, she pressed her well-crafted speech in Henry Harvey's ear. Waning in strength against her constant barrage of sweetly stated demands and ultimatums, he caved.

Languishing in the compromised state of an illness that lingered for months, Henry Harvey relinquished Albert's inheritance to Sidney. As the springtime came, and the season for sowing arrived, Henry Harvey passed away.

The breach was complete, and the inheritance usurped. Relationships broken, Albert Austin did his best to move on, but the trauma remained. Bitterness set in, and life would be tainted for his own children, and grandchildren to come.

Repairing The Breach

Shortly after placing my name securely into Father's hands, I embarked on another phase of research into my ancestry. Large gaps existed on the paternal historical account, and I held little knowledge of spiritual import flowing through the family. I felt like a black sheep among my immediate family members, seemingly alone in my born again status.

Following a directive from the Lord, I set out to inquire of the Lord concerning my generational inheritance.

Although the starting point was stark, Father quickly led me to the first discovered blessing: my paternal generations were filled with gospel influence—a long and powerful history of ministry influence. My faith hadn't sprung from thin air, I was simply disconnected from the generational knowledge of Covenant connection. Someone, somewhere, on our family line had prayed, taking hold of the Covenant blessing: you, and your children, even unto the third and fourth generation. The commanded blessing of Deuteronomy was in effect, and available–upon the removal of the covenant breach-point.

What wasn't so obvious was the breach point. Family anecdotes were few and far between–including some items that just weren't talked about. I'd grown up with a sense that information was being buried, without knowing why.

Symptoms of a breach were very evident. Even though I'd invested significant time to overcome besetting sins, and had overcome many issues, the lingering effect of a breach remained. I determined to employ the 'geas evidence' list to frame the symptoms in a new light, hoping to understand the hindrances to my purpose. Among those I'd studiously listed: birth by Cesarean section, the Stockholm effect, psychological restriction of movement, and repeated attempts to move into a greater measure of calling. These now topped the list of hindrances to my purpose as a messenger, a teacher and preacher of the Gospel.

With the discovery of the broken promise surrounding inheritance, years of struggle and question unexpectedly gave way to an effortless exchange of details that brought the various shattered pieces of my upbringing into full view. I now had clarity on familial behavior patterns present in my forefathers. A veritable "connect the dots" was presented to me, and I now held the key!

The enemy had staged an illegal coup the against our family. Using the sound of our name, he had targeted the Scriptural principle of inheritance, he managed to thwart a binding verbal agreement between father and son.

> *The Lord, The Lord God, merciful and gracious, longsuffering, and abundant in goodness and truth, keeping mercy for thousands, forgiving iniquity and transgression and sin, and that will by no means clear the guilty; <u>visiting the iniquity of the fathers upon the children, and upon the children's children, unto the third and to the fourth generation.</u>*
>
> — Exodus 34:6-7 KJV

The father-son duo was of my third and fourth generation. The father, my great-great grand, fourth generation; the son, my great-grandfather, third generation.

Theft, independence, and use of personal influence could be directly tied to the illegal action of the enemy against the father-son bond.

Now that the transgression of a covenant principle was revealed, I could approach the Mercy Seat. From the position of prayer, I would lift up the sin of the previous generations, and ask that forgiveness be applied to the breach of trust. I requested access to the heavenly courts, to file an injunction against the thief,[8] and to make a demand of return of that which had been seized–not simply an inheritance lost–rather, honor and faithfulness; trust and fidelity.

When [the thief] he is found, he must repay sevenfold; He must give all the substance of his house.

— Proverbs 6:31 KJV

7

THE SOUND REDEEMED

We've heard true stories from our fathers about our rich heritage. We will continue to tell our children and not hide from the rising generation the great marvels of our God—His miracles and power that have brought us all this far

For perpetuity God's ways will be passed down from one generation to the next, even to those not yet born.

In this way, every generation will have a living faith in the laws of life and will never forget the faithful ways of God.

By following His ways, they will break the past bondage of their fickle fathers, who were a stubborn and rebellious generation ...

— Psalm 78:3-8 TPT

Repairing the breach in my generational line led to the discovery of many wondrous things. Of these, two stand out from the rest. First, shortly after I prayed concerning the broken inheritance matter of the fourth generation, my father initiated the creation of his will. At his action, he informed my sister and I that we were included in his consideration. He was under no compulsion to inform us of his inclusion, yet the action further informed me that Father God had repaired the previous breach.

Second, the discovery that a great number of my forefathers were faith-filled ministers of the Gospel came into full view. Apostolic pioneers; preachers and teachers filled the gaps of the sound of my family line! Our family name continues in reknown, having impacted the nation with the Gospel. One man in my lineage in particular was a noted orator. Tracing his life and career in the faith, I came to know that he had spent time as an evangelist, not far from where I reside at the time of this writing. He returned to his home state and promptly took up the preaching circuit of the community, and closed his days as the president of a regional Christian college. Suddenly my gift mix made sense in light of legacy.

It was the element of sound that led to these discoveries. Names, once hidden from memory, surged forward, reestablishing identity, purpose, and destiny in a new generation–*in me*. This is the handiwork of God.

> *For this cause I bow my knees unto the Father, from whom every family in heaven and on earth is named...*
>
> — Ephesians 3:14-15 KJV

The Name Speaks

When THE NAME spoke your name before the foundation of the world, identity, purpose, and destiny were released into the substance of your being.

Held, suspended, until the appointed time of history, your conception indicated His purpose for you had arrived. Your days were fashioned and prepared. At your birth, your name was recorded and spoken, impinging upon the realm of the earth with the impact of the King. Your birth produced His opportunity to govern in this realm, through the element of sound.

What is the meaning of your name? What purpose did Father intend for you to release, as He named you thus?

Is your name in any way held captive, perhaps through no fault of your own, but because of generational iniquity?

Were the sound of your name to be delivered out of the hand of the enemy, transformed by the Gospel of the Kingdom, how would the trajectory of your destiny shift?

Were the ownership of your name restored to the Father, what transformation would take place?

When The Name speaks, He speaks through your name.

GLOSSARY

Chapter 1

1. **Elemental Sound:** Sound waves as the integral building blocks of all creation
2. **Exegesis:** The critical explanation or interpretation of a religious text
3. **PaRDes:** A Hebraic method of interpretation, set in four parts
4. **Poiçma:** Greek word for workmanship, to produce; poetry
5. **The Name:** One expression among many to describe the Godhead

Chapter 2

1. **Authority:** The power derived from the influence of character, produces credibility, respectability, and dignity; the aptitude or right to act, or give orders, such as the rule of a prince superimposed upon subjects or parents over children
2. **Beryith:** Hebrew word for covenant that describes the act of cutting, or passing between pieces of flesh
3. **Character:** Understood as a mark, made by cutting or engraving, either by pen or stylus, on paper or other material; peculiar attributes which he possesses, such as a reputation; a

4. **Covenant:** Considered legal language, a covenant transcends time and space. It remains in effect until it is fulfilled or overturned. A demonstration of the measure of His faithfulness **Nature:** Born, produced; the essential qualities or attributes of a thing; temperament, what sort, or particular predisposition one owns
5. **Onoma:** Greek word for 'nature, character, and authority'; includes one's rank, excellence or deeds; to become acquainted with, to know

Chapter 3

1. **Geas:** To hold one prisoner, based upon the failure to complete a vow or pledge
2. **Genius-loci:** The spirit of a place

Chapter 6

1. **breach:** a broken place, particularly a wall once positioned as a protection; The violation of a law; the violation or non-fulfillment of a contract; the non-performance of a moral duty; non-performance of duty being a breach of obligation, as well as a positive transgression or violation

NOTES

1. The Name

1. The American Heritage® Dictionary of the English Language, 5th Edition.
2. Souter, A. (1917). A Pocket Lexicon to the Greek New Testament
3. The Abridged Brown-Driver-Briggs Hebrew-English Lexicon of the Old Testament: from A Hebrew and English Lexicon of the Old Testament by Francis Brown, S.R. Driver and Charles Briggs,
4. Name Covenant, Invitation to Friendship, Anne Hamilton
5. God's Poetry, Anne Hamilton, 2015

2. The Name and The Covenant

1. https://www.blueletterbible.org/lang/lexicon/lexicon.cfm?Strongs=G1097 Accessed 3/26/21
2. http://webstersdictionary1828.com/Dictionary/nature Accessed 3/26/21
3. http://webstersdictionary1828.com/Dictionary/character Accessed 3/26/21
4. Paul speaks of this in layered fashion in 2 Corinthians 10:6
5. Mike Wazowski, Monsters, inc., 2001 Walt Disney Pictures, Pixar Entertainment
6. https://www.blueletterbible.org/lang/lexicon/lexicon.cfm?Strongs=H1285&t=KJV Accessed 3/26/21
7. Mark 10:8

3. Whose Name is it Anyway?

1. Numbers 6:27
2. https://www.abarim-publications.com/Meaning/Jeremiah.html
3. God's Poetry, Anne Hamilton
4. Name Covenant, Invitation to Friendship, Anne Hamilton
5. God's Poetry The Identity and Destiny Encoded In Your Name, Anne Hamilton

5. A Name In Distress

1. *The Holy Bible: King James Version.* (2009) Logos Research Systems, Inc.
2. https://www.abarim-publications.com/Meaning/Zaphenath-paneah.html#.X-khoelKjOQ
3. https://www.abarim-publications.com/Meaning/Asenath.html#.X-kj9OlKjOQ
4. Genesis 35:16-18
5. Jamieson, R., Fausset, A. R., & Brown, D. (1997). *Commentary Critical and Explanatory on the Whole Bible* (Vol. 1, p. 251). Oak Harbor, WA
6. See Numbers 3:3-16
7. https://www.abarim-publications.com/Meaning/Jabez.html#.X-lqjulKjOQ
8. See Genesis 28:20

6. Repairing The Breach

1. http://www.webstersdictionary1828.com/Dictionary/breach
2. John 8:12
3. Name Covenant, Invitation to Friendship, Anne Hamilton
4. I discuss this in depth in my teaching Basics of Ekklesia Intercession.
5. Isaiah 28:12
6. Proverbs 13:22 KJV
7. This book contains a summary of my journey of discovery. A written work in progress, surrounding Moses' encounter with the daughters of Zelophehad expands upon this summary with greater detail.
8. John 10:10: The thief comes only to steal, kill and destroy.

ABOUT THE AUTHOR

Angela Broussard, in her professional capacity, serves as Director of Wells of SouthGate, a Five-Fold Training and Equipping Center on the Mississippi Gulf Coast. From this administrative leadership position, she functions in grace-flow as a Teacher, Prophetic Intercessor, as well as Strategic Co-Lead in Topographical Intercession. Angela is a contributing and active member of the regional Ekklesia, apostolically led, with all five of the grace flows of Kingdom Leadership in operation.

Living as a Word-centric, Angela has impacted the lives of others through her empowering and Spirit-led teaching. Graced with a capacity to articulate the living status of the Word of God, students of the King have found themselves walking in ever-deepening measures of maturity, reflecting the nature, character, and authority of Christ.

Five children and eight grandchildren endow the Broussard family, as do the five donkeys, one horse, two dogs and numerous chickens. The combination leads to never-a-dull moment, with plenty of room for laughter to accompany them. The Lord's behest marked their decision to put down roots in the rudder of the nation.

Angela is commissioned and appointed in alignment with Network Ekklesia International (NEI) and Wells of SouthGate. Angela is preparing to receive her Masters in Kingdom Leadership via Kingdom Leadership International, Jacksonville, FL.

Angela is available for ministry engagements, speaking appointments, workshops and conferences. For more information, please contact the administration at silvercornerstone@gmail.com

www.silvercornerstone.com

DOORS GATES & THRESHOLDS SERIES

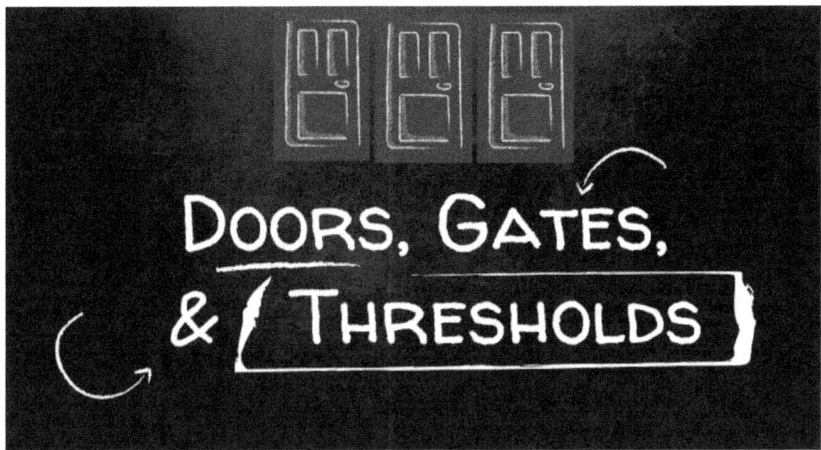

Hearing Him call your name is but the beginning! When your identity is clear, your purpose comes to the forefront, and the King hands out your assignment. From the moment you engage, you'll be asked to complete His instructions in a manner that reflects His Kingdom. Decisions await your execution, so you'll want to be equipped for each juncture with the understanding of how His Covenant undergirds your travels. Meet wisdom along the way, and make her your valued companion.

The Doors Gates Thresholds Series is available through Kingdom Leadership Institute Gulf Coast. Semester by semester, be equipped to identify and properly dismantle ancient fortresses that limit the expansion of the Kingdom of God.

THE DESTINY SERIES
BY REBECCA D BENNETT

The Destiny Series is a strategic training designed to help you discover the who and the why that you are. You are designed to become a great leader that God intended you to be, and you can reach your maximum potential in the ministry that the Lord Jesus gave to every person (Matthew 28:19)

The Destiny Series will help you understand and apply the essential foundations of your vision: having the character of Christ (Following Jesus) and reproducing it in other people (Building leaders).

D1: IDENTITY

D2: PURPOSE

D3: AUTHORITY

D4: LEGACY

This dynamic and interactive series is available for individual or group study, as well as an author-led course. To learn more, visit www.rebeccadbennett.com

Wells of SouthGate is a training, equipping, and activating center serving the Mississippi Gulf Coast. Our passion is to see each person matured to fulfill our God-given dreams and destiny, to become a flourishing, contributing member of their society. For more information, visit our website:

www.wellsofsouthgate.com

3Trees Publishing was born, the result of the architectural build out of Wells of SouthGate. Following the blueprints for the region, 3Trees Publishing serves to reconnect creatives with their Kingdom calling by supplying a framework of excellence for all printed work. This endeavor reintroduces and reconstitutes the original intent and design for the Spanish West Florida Territory and beyond. Let the expression of your purpose be revealed as you prepare legacy for those who come after. For more information, contact us at 3Treespublishing@gmail.com.

Kingdom Leadership Institute Gulf Coast

Making Excellence Visible

The Leadership Institute of choice prepares you for leadership in the Kingdom of God. The strategy of KLI GC is individualized. Your leadership training can begin at any level of spiritual and ministry maturity. We start where you are with what you do. As one can function in any aspect of culture, once taught to function in kingdom culture, the Institute educates and prepares students for any arena of occupation. We honor kingdom leaders from every walk of life. Students come from many professions and occupations.

Learning Outcomes

Jesus called people to new life. He then turned kingdom people into kingdom leaders. Kingdom influence expanded through these kingdom leaders. Partnered with KLI Jacksonville, our course intensives develop mature individuals to impact the current culture with Kingdom culture. Whatever your sphere of influence, your effectiveness will increase exponentially, as you engage in the values and principles that reflect the King. Determine today to engage your life's work at the starting gate of Kingdom Leadership Institute Gulf Coast. For more information or to enroll, contact us at kligulfcoast@gmail.com.

Designs x Laura is a brand and service for helping others find and interpret their vision. Whether you offer a product or service, are new or established in your field or maybe don't know what the next step is for you, Laura is here for you. From creating your logo to web design and even providing successful tips for how to efficiently expand and market your business; you will begin to see your vision manifest before your eyes.

Web Design, Graphic Design, and Business Consulting services. Visit www.designsxlaura.com/services for a list of all services provided. If you don't see a specific marketing need, feel free to reach out and our team to discuss your innovative ideas.

www.ingramcontent.com/pod-product-compliance
Lightning Source LLC
Chambersburg PA
CBHW071030080526
44587CB00015B/2562